Shale Oil

A history of the industry in the Lothians

Guthrie Hutton

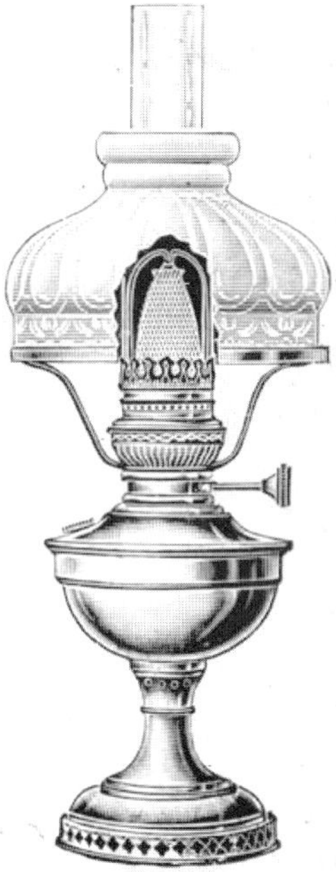

The chalked board tells the story; these men worked at the Oakbank paraffin refinery.

Text © Guthrie Hutton, 2010.
First published in the United Kingdom, 2010,
by Stenlake Publishing Ltd.
Telephone: 01290 551122
www.stenlake.co.uk

ISBN 9781840335026

Acknowledgements

I have been fascinated by the shale oil industry for a long time, but also puzzled by the lack of recognition given to it and to James Young, the man who started it all. This little book has therefore given me an opportunity to highlight the man and the industry, and I am grateful to a number of people who have assisted in that endeavour. Sybil Cavanagh at West Lothian Library Headquarters at Blackburn has been a big help with research and providing pictures. The Almond Valley Heritage Trust at Livingston has not only a splendid display on the industry, but also an excellent collection of pictures and ephemera and I am grateful to them for allowing me to use material from it. Hazel Marjoribanks, David Noon, Gareth Burgess and Tom Henderson kindly provided or gave permission for the use of pictures, as did fellow scribe Ian Brodie for the picture on page 46. I must also pay tribute to the work done by David Kerr whose books and articles on the industry are a collective tour-de-force.

Further Reading

Cadell, H. M., *The Rocks of West Lothian*, 1925.
Cavanagh, Sybil, (editor), *Pumpherston: The Story of a Shale Oil Village*, 2002.
Findlay, Alastair, *Shale Voices*, 1999.
Geological Survey, Scotland, *The Oil Shales of the Lothians*, 1927.
Hutton, Guthrie, *Mining the Lothians*, 1998.
Kerr, David, *Shale Oil: Scotland*, 1991.
Kerr, David, *Tarbrax*, 2002.
Patullo, Barbara and Marie, *Hail Philpstoun's Queen*, 2004.
Redwood, Iltyd, *Mineral Oils and Their By-Products*, 1897.

Right: Tarbrax, just over the Lanarkshire border, may have seen a few wild nights during the boom times, but not perhaps the level of glamour implied by this Edwardian postcard.

Introduction

In 1847 James Young, a chemist from Glasgow, was working in Manchester for the chemical manufacturer Charles Tennant & Co. when his attention was drawn to a naturally occurring flow of oily liquid in a coal mine at Alfreton in Derbyshire and he was given leave to exploit its commercial possibilities. He isolated paraffin wax, and created a machine oil for the cotton mills, but after two years the oil stopped flowing and Young had some thinking to do.

Convinced the coal had been heated in the geological past to create the oil, Young attempted to repeat the process using samples from other mines. A cannel coal, so called because it burned with a bright, candle-like flame, from Torbanehill, near Bathgate, encouraged Young to return to Scotland where he drew up a patent to cover his process of distilling oil from coal, came to an agreement with the mine operator for supplies of the mineral, and in 1851 set up the world's first oil refinery at Bathgate in partnership with lawyer and financier Edward W. Binney and chemist Edward Meldrum.

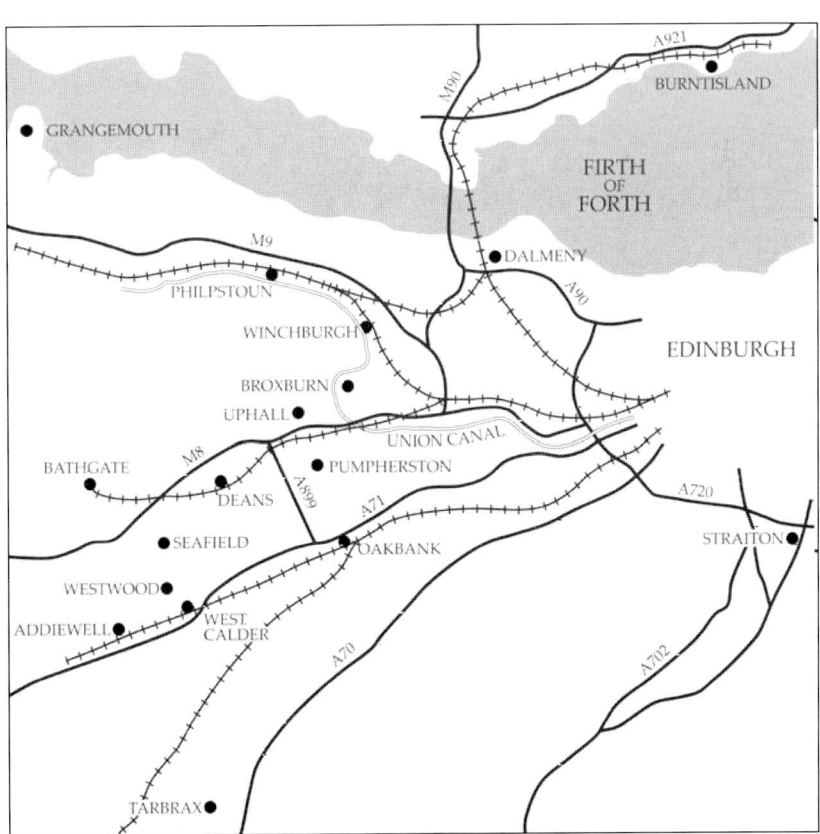

Trouble arose when the landowner, irked by the low royalty he was getting for a highly priced mineral, challenged the mine operator over its true nature. Searching for a name, the Lord President of the Court of Session called it Torbane Mineral, and although the court ruled that it was coal, later analysis showed that the mineral was unique, and closer to being a very rich shale than to coal. Shale is the volcanic mud and ash from the bed of a lagoon compressed into sedimentary rock in the Carboniferous geological period 350 million years ago. Only those shales that also contain a high percentage of vegetable matter yield oil and in Britain they only occur in West Lothian and in small pockets of Mid Lothian and Fife.

The court's decision, that the Bathgate mineral was coal, may have favoured Young, but he was soon having to confront a more pressing geological reality, the imminent exhaustion of the mine. He had started to experiment with shale and it was already being used to produce oil at Broxburn, so taking a lease on a large shalefield at Addiewell, he started to build a new works there in 1864. His refining patents expired in the same year and those for distillation applied only to coal, so he was now facing competition on all fronts as numerous small companies also set up oil works across the Lothians and beyond.

Of greater significance was that the Americans struck oil in 1859 and without the need to retort shale could refine it more cheaply. If Young had not started up his oil works when he did the Americans would probably have got into the market first and there might never have been a Scottish shale oil industry, but there was and for the next 100 years it was sustained by constant improvement and innovation in both plant and product development, and a willingness to engage in fierce competition for market share.

Between the 1860s and 1890s over 100 small shale oil companies tried their luck, but most lacked capital or expertise and either went out of business or were taken over, so that by the end of the nineteenth century there were only six large companies. That number had been reduced to five by the start of the First World War, but technical innovation had reached its zenith and those early years of the twentieth century were golden ones for the industry.

After the First World War a rising demand for oil was met by more and cheaper imports, an irresolvable dilemma that confronted the shale industry while its own costs were going up. A common management company, Scottish Oils, was set up to co-ordinate the activities of the five companies. It was a subsidiary of the partly state-owned Anglo Persian Oil Co. Ltd. which later became the Anglo Iranian Oil Co. and then British Petroleum (BP), so the government was now taking an interest, but outwardly kept its distance as the economic and labour troubles of the 1920s assailed the industry. There was disruption when shale miners tried to maintain parity with higher wages in the coal industry and a major strike in 1925 preceded wage reductions and significant closures, but in the late 1920s the industry began to receive official support when the government introduced preferential tax exemptions.

In 1932 Scottish Oils assumed full control of what was now seen as a strategically important indigenous industry. A couple of years later the government guaranteed the continuance of duty preferences for home produced fuel and extended these measures in the late 1930s. This gave the industry the confidence to invest in new mines, and a new crude oil works, that saw production increase through the Second World War.

Peace brought a return of shale's old problem of having to combat rapid growth in imported oil, while its own costs and consequent losses were rising. The government resisted pressure to extend financial assistance and in the early 1960s, when it announced the removal of duty preferences to meet international free trade commitments, closures became inevitable. The heroic, unequal struggle of competing against free-flowing oil wells ceased in 1962.

Shale workers housing at Pumpherston showing the distinctive castellated sculleries attached to the cottage fronts.

4

James Young was born in 1811 in Glasgow. He studied chemistry in evening classes at the Andersonian Institute, now Strathclyde University, and became a lecturer there and then in London before leaving academia in 1838 to pursue a career in industry. As a result of his fortuitous move into oil production he was able to draw up patents that established the principles of oil refining that still hold good today. He guarded those patents jealously and pursued violations in courts on both sides of the Atlantic. Many of the words he used in those patents, like cracking, have become the common parlance of the industry. Known as Paraffin Young, he was in effect the world's first oil man and amassed a considerable fortune before retiring in 1871. Toward the end of his life he moved to an estate near Wemyss Bay on the Clyde Coast, where he died in 1883. Before that, while working at Addiewell and in early retirement, he lived in this mansion, Limefield House, built in 1804 near West Calder.

With the Bathgate plant's future as an oil refinery fading, Young bought out his partners and concentrated on developing the Addiewell works. When it was completed in 1866 Young sold his interests in it to a limited company, but remained as the general manager with a seat on the board of directors. The new business, Young's Paraffin Light and Mineral Oil Company Limited, became one of the largest and longest lasting of the Lothian oil companies. It retained the Bathgate plant, which was used for various subsidiary processes, and also operated works at Uphall and Winchburgh, but Addiewell was its principal concern. Thought to have been the largest oil works in the world in its early days it was used as a crude oil works, refinery, sulphuric acid works and candle making factory. It closed in 1956, as did the original works at Bathgate which had latterly been used to produce sulphuric acid.

Scenery-Home Manufacture.-

The oil works had a huge impact on what had been a quiet rural location, and nowhere was the effect of this unfettered industrialisation greater than on this little smallholding, which predated the works. Known as Bridge End, it acquired another name, Clash-me-Doon, which has been artistically penned below the picture along with the description above it of the scenery being of Home Manufacture. This is all wryly cynical because the hill behind the house is not a natural feature, but is the bing of spent shale waste created by the Addiewell works. The bing also curled round either side of the house and the picture has been taken from a railway used to take hutches of spent shale to the bings, so the house was literally surrounded. With about eighty per cent of the volume of mined shale going on the bing, it grew like an alien force from a science fiction story, inexorably swamping everything in its path including the wee smallholding, which it did eventually clash doon.

-Clash-me-doon-

The foundation stone of the Addiewell complex was laid in 1864 by the African explorer and missionary David Livingstone, who was a friend of Young from their student days. Young provided funding for Livingstone's adventures, but it is the explorer that Scotland lionises and not the man who created the wealth that made it all possible! The explorer did, however, leave his mark on the area. He planted a tree at Limefield House when he stayed there with Young and this main street through Addiewell was known as Livingstone Street. Young's Paraffin Light and Mineral Oil Company owned 360 single roomed or two apartment houses in the village. Built either in rows or tenements like these they came out badly in a 1914 report on shale workers housing. The occupants of 300 houses had to share twelve privvies which were described as objectionable, sewage was allowed to flow in open channels and ashpits for rubbish disposal, sited within twenty yards of the houses, were regarded as a positive pestilence in the summer and at all times a danger to health.

The company was also criticised in the 1914 report into shale workers' housing for not providing wash houses at Addiewell and sticking a few clothes poles here and there in the back courts. There were only seventeen standpipes to supply water for the entire village. At West Calder, where the company owned 159 houses, there were four standpipes, no wash houses, no sculleries and unsatisfactory privvies. Two thirds of these houses had only one room with a brick floor and if the tenants wanted this replaced with a timber floor they had to do much of the heavy work themselves and pay more in rent. The larger of these pictures shows some Young Company housing in a development at the west end of West Calder known as the Happy Land, an odd name perhaps and yet life in such dwellings was often happy in the sense of shared community and togetherness. The smaller picture, of sadly poor quality, shows some rows at Gavieside acquired by the company when it took over the West Calder Oil Company in 1879. Even in 1914 they were regarded as so old and poor they ought to be condemned.

When in 1934 the government guaranteed the preferential price for home produced fuel for ten years, Scottish Oils responded by opening a new pit, Burngrange, about a mile from the Addiewell works. Two fourteen foot diameter shafts were sunk to a depth of 468 feet and lined with bricks made from spent shale (see page 27). The principal shaft, No. 1, could raise 1,000 tons of shale in an eight hour shift and was also the means of access and egress for the men. The pit worked a 650 acre field of the highly productive Dunnet Seam, ten foot thick, but not flat. It fell away from the shaft, to the west, at an angle of 1 in 4.5, and rose to the east before dropping away again. Power for the all-electric pit was supplied by Addiewell works power station. In the picture on the left a miner is seen using an electric drill to make a shot hole; on the right a diesel locomotive hauls hutches to the pit bottom. Burngrange went into production in 1936, but in January 1947 the naked light from a mine worker's carbide lamp ignited some gas and set off the shale industry's worst pit disaster. Methane gas, or firedamp as it was known in the mining industry, was present in many shale mines, and there were explosions: five died at Hayscraigs Mine, Broxburn, in 1882, two at Pumpherston No. 4 Mine in 1902 and three men were killed at Philpstoun No. 5 Mine in 1907, and there were others although casualties were mercifully few. The big difference between coal and shale mines was that coal dust could explode if it became airborne, contributing significantly to the severity of disasters, whereas shale dust was inert and tended to damp down explosions. At Burngrange, once the gas was ignited the flame spread into waste workings where accumulations of gas exploded, setting off fires that burned timber supports and brought down the roof. Rescuers took four days to reach the fifteen trapped men, one of whom had been killed in the initial explosion and the others all poisoned by white damp (carbon monoxide gas) which was usually present after a mine explosion. Burngrange Pit closed in 1956.

In 1938 the government increased the duty preference for home produced fuel and extended the guarantee for twelve years. Encouraged by this, Scottish Oils set about building a new crude oil works at Westwood, near West Calder, the first to be commissioned for nearly forty years. The state-of-the-art complex could process over 1,000 tons of shale a day in 104 retorts. The ultimate development of this highly specialised piece of equipment, these were contained in two 90 foot high structures known as benches, on the right of this picture. The conveyor that delivered shale to them can be seen rising from the buildings on the left where the crushers were situated. The shale was distributed to the individual retorts by shuttle conveyors running along the tops of the benches. Westwood opened in 1941 and closed 21 years later having created the industry's most iconic landmark, the five sisters bing.

Five miles from West Calder, on the high ground just across the Lanarkshire border, was the most southerly shale works, Tarbrax. Although the man who set it up in 1868, E. W. Fernie, died before it was completed, it worked for about five years before being abandoned. The British Oil and Candle Company purchased the works and mineral lease in 1880, but was taken over three years later by the Lanark Oil Company. They invested heavily, but lost heavily too and sold out for a pittance in 1886. Next to try its hand was the Caledonian Mineral Oil Company Ltd. which took over in 1889 and after they put more money in the works, mines and village went into liquidation in 1897. It was an English company, so it reregistered in Scotland, rearranged its finances and kept going until 1903. Hopes had thus been raised and dashed here for 35 years, but some people still believed there was potential and in 1904 the newly formed Tarbrax Oil Company started the process of reconstruction. Building work is seen under way in this picture taken before Christmas 1904 (snow can be a familiar sight in a Tarbrax winter).

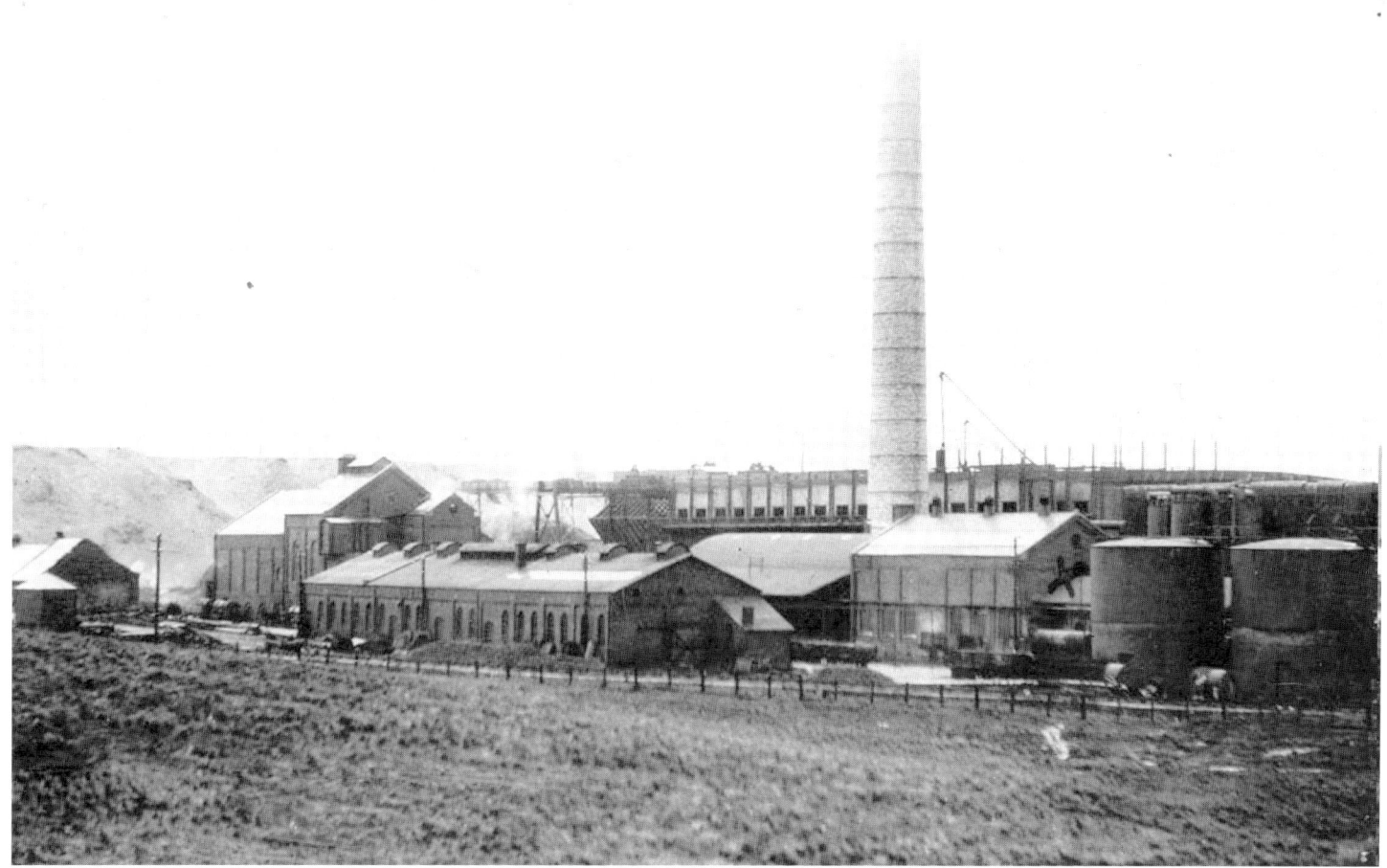

What marked the Tarbrax Oil Company out from its predecessors was that it was promoted by William Fraser of the Pumpherston Oil Company and he was supported by other men who knew the oil business well. They knew that the principal mineral contained in the lease, the rich Fells seam of shale, if mined economically and processed in the latest retorts, should yield oil profitably. A key element of the rebuilt works and mines was electricity. The power station can be seen between the chimney and the tanks on the right of this picture and beside it in the construction picture on the facing page. Tarbrax became a profitable concern for the first time in its history and in 1913 the Pumpherston Oil Company took over the whole operation, but the stresses that caused the industry to contract after the First World War had a severe effect on Tarbrax. A strike in 1921 over a non-union man at one of the pits, and the national coal miners' strike that year, shut down the operation. Production ceased in 1926 and the works was dismantled the following year.

When the oil men came to Tarbrax there was no village, no roads, no houses, just a bare, windswept slope. However, as each failed company moved out they left behind a bigger village than the one they started with. From a handful of dwellings in the late 1860s and early 1870s, the village grew to over 80 houses and a population in excess of 500 in the early 1890s. The number of houses had almost doubled by 1900 and in 1914, when the Royal Commission on Housing in Scotland was collecting evidence, it found that 1,571 people lived in 296 houses. The ownership of most of these houses passed from one oil company to the next, but when the works closed in 1926, the Pumpherston Oil Company, anxious to remove a financial burden, cleared most of the tenants and demolished two thirds of the houses. The remaining buildings were sold. The pictures show the village looking south from the old bing (upper) and (lower) four houses erected for Tarbrax Oil Company managers and officials.

Co-operative Buildings, Tarbrax.

Initially Tarbrax was served by a company store and, for a few years, a small local co-operative society, but in 1905 the Tarbrax Oil Company encouraged the West Calder Co-operative Society to take over the old company store premises. The society, which had been formed in 1875, was arguably the most significant in the shale oil area. Their Tarbrax shop was so successful that in 1907 the society took over the adjacent hall as its grocery department and set up a butchery in the original shop which is seen here in close proximity to the old bing, on the right. The oil company built a new institute and hall to replace the one taken over by the society, but the co-op remained at the heart of Tarbrax village life and central to one of the social highlights of year, the childrens' gala day. Children formed up outside the store and, headed by a band from West Calder, paraded through the village to a field where they took part in races and games, and ate buns from the co-op bakery - great!

The Oakbank Oil Company was formed in 1869, taking over the works started in 1863 by the Mid-Calder Oil Company which had been set up to exploit the McLean shales, a name given locally to the seams known elsewhere as the Broxburn shales. Two major advances in retort technology emanated from the Oakbank works. The first of these, designed in 1873 by works manager N. M. Henderson, significantly improved efficiency and yield and was rapidly adopted elsewhere, but no sooner had the new retorts become almost universal than a further advance was made by Oakbank's chief chemist George T. Beilby and William Young of the Clippens Oil Company at Straiton. Developed in 1882, these new Young and Beilby retorts quickly superseded Henderson retorts at Oakbank and elsewhere. After a long and successful existence, Oakbank refinery and works closed in 1931.

In 1894 a fire, thought to have been caused by a spark from the pug locomotive, broke out in the vicinity of a bleaching house and spread to buildings where barrels were filled with oil. The fire moved so quickly that the 20 men who operated the works' own fire engine, lost a line of hose before they were ready to fight the flames. The Edinburgh brigade was summoned, but sent only one fire engine instead of the two requested. Luckily a change in the wind direction took the fire away from the retorts and condensers, and the naphtha tanks which, had they exploded, could have destroyed the entire works. Seven storage tanks containing £20,000 worth of oil were protected by a high wall, but a 30 foot high stack of empty barrels was consumed as was a train of railway wagons on the loading bank. As the fire advanced across the site it reached the dirty pond, a waste water settling pond, but instead of being halted by the water, the flames took hold of the oily surface and leaped 60 to 80 feet into the air, an apocalyptic scene likened by one onlooker to Dante's Inferno. The blaze was eventually contained and burned itself out and, although badly damaged, the works was able to keep going thanks to a good insurance policy and the survival of the main production plant.

When, during the 1894 fire, the change of wind direction saved the main part of the Oakbank works, it also saved the village which was only 60 yards away at its closest point. The houses, about 200 in all, built of brick and arranged in rows, were mostly of two apartments, room and kitchen or kitchen and attic, although there were a few single room houses. Some of the buildings were two storey tenements with six, room and kitchen, houses on the ground floor and six above. Initially there were standpipes for water and communal privvies, but these were superseded about 1914 when toilets and sculleries were installed in small brick extensions to the fronts of houses. These are evident in the upper picture which shows the same houses as are shown on the front cover in a picture that predates the scullery extensions. The lower picture shows the posh end of the village, although such a term is clearly relative. The village also boasted an institute, bowling green and football pitch.

The location of the principal shales was initially determined by outcrops that appeared on the surface or in the sides of valleys, the seams lying in undulating waves at varying depths having been distorted in the geological past. Volcanic heat and other forces had affected the quality and thickness of the mineral in places so that it was never just a simple task of knowing where and how good the shale was; it had to be found and proved before any mine was opened. Drills were employed to explore the strata and the material they brought to the surface was examined and tested. Some early drills used a chisel-like tip that penetrated the ground with a percussive action, but this shattered the rock it passed though, making the samples it obtained hard to analyse. The better tool was a diamond tipped bore that brought core samples to the surface. One such hand-operated drill, used by a contractor from Ayrshire, is seen here in the Mid-Calder area with some core samples displayed beside it.

AERIAL RAILWAY, DEDRIDGE, MID. CALDER

The Oakbank Company opened a new mine at Dedridge in 1909 and built this aerial ropeway. to transport the shale between the mine and the oil works. The bridge-like structure seen here was erected to protect the main Edinburgh road from shale falling out of the buckets as they swayed along overhead. The ropeway system was of German design and manufacture and so when war broke out in 1914 the maker's plates were removed to avoid embarrassment. During the First World War the local highways authority tried to stop the Oakbank Company from transporting miners in motor charabancs to another new mine at Westwood. They feared that this would damage the roads, but such concerns were dismissed by the government's Director of Inland Transport because the need for oil was vital to the war effort. Post-war decline was felt quickly in the Oakbank mines with Dedridge closing in 1919 and although local men were re-employed at Westwood, men who lived elsewhere lost their jobs.

OAKBANK OIL Co's WORKS, AERIAL ROPEWAY TERMINAL

With the aerial ropeway mechanism in the foreground, the Oakbank works is seen here from the bing, looking south. Behind the works, to the right, is the viaduct carrying the Caledonian Railway across the Linnhouse Water. Originally the Caledonian's line ran up from Carlisle to Carstairs and branched to Edinburgh and Glasgow, and while this gave the company a route between the cities it was much longer than the one via Falkirk operated by the rival North British Railway. In July 1869 the Caledonian opened a new section of track between Cleland in Lanarkshire and the Calders, cutting out the long detour to Carstairs. This gave them a more competitive route, but it also provided a line from which numerous mines and industries in Lanarkshire and West Lothian could be served. Oakbank and Addiewell were both adjacent to the main line, but other mines and works were served by branch lines snaking out across the shalefield. The North British also laid tracks in from the north as the rival railway companies vied for a share of the lucrative shale oil business.

In 1883 William Fraser resigned as manager of the oil works at Uphall and, with his brother Archibald, leased the minerals on Pumpherston Estate. There were five seams of shale pushed close to the surface by an anticline, an upward arching of the geological strata. Too deep to work elsewhere, these shales gave a good yield of oil, but a better one of ammonia. The Pumpherston Oil Company was formed in November and a start made on sinking mines and building the new works. It was hoped to be producing oil by the autumn of 1884, in time to meet winter demand, but the works manager struggled to get the plant ready and resigned. William Fraser himself took over and got the works into production before another manager was appointed. The new man also struggled and was sacked when deteriorating relationships with the board and staff threatened the company's future. It was a reflection of how hard it was to find people with the experience and range of skills needed to set up and run such large and complex plants. But after reorganising its management structures, the company did find the right man, James Bryson, who was to have a major impact on the industry.

Ten years after formation of the Pumpherston Oil Company the works employed 700 people and covered 23 acres of ground. Four benches of Young and Beilby retorts were processing 600 tons of shale a day, more than double the initially intended quantity, and the refinery could deal with 120,000 gallons of crude oil a week. Through the 1890s the company continued to expand, acquiring the works of the Bathgate Oil Company at Seafield and the West Lothian Oil Company at Deans. By the end of the century it had become the third largest oil company and at the outbreak of the First World War, having absorbed the Tarbrax Company, it was the largest. It accounted for over half of the entire industry when Scottish Oils took over in 1919. Crude oil production at Pumpherston stopped in 1925 and it became the sole refinery for shale oil and remained in operation until 1964, refining oil from England for a couple of years after the Scottish industry had ceased operations. A detergent plant established on the site after the Second World War remained in operation until 1993.

When James Bryson arrived as manager of the Pumpherston works in 1887, he brought with him engineering skills learned in some of Scotland's largest shipbuilding and iron works and he applied these to retort design. He increased the diameter of retorts and made them longer. A mechanism at the foot regularly removed small quantities of spent shale so that the contents moved downward continuously and in the tapered shape also shifted sideways to be evenly exposed to heat ranging from 1,800° at the bottom of the surrounding flues to 1,000° at the top. Much of the heat was generated by burning gases produced in the process. The retorts, grouped four to a furnace and with up to 64 in a bench, were contained in a structure about 60 feet tall. This was kept clear of the ground on columns that allowed hutches to run underneath and remove the spent shale, while hutches at the top kept the loading hoppers topped up. Much more efficient than their predecessors, these new retorts brought shale oil's costs closer to those of natural oil. The big companies moved rapidly to re-equip, but smaller ones, unable to meet the rebuilding costs and thus share in the better returns, went out of business.

It is easy to imagine oil flowing out of a tap at the foot of the retort, but it wasn't like that. Steam was injected continuously into the retort and as it swept up through the hot mineral it collected the mixture of vapours and gases and was taken off by pipes in the neck of the retort. This was just the start of complex chemical processes whereby the retorted products were separated into crude oil, ammonia liquor and naphtha. The crude oil was then distilled and refined to make a variety of oils, paraffin, wax and latterly petrol and diesel. The ammonia liquor went to make sulphate of ammonia, a highly profitable fertiliser. Treated and distilled the naphtha was used for spirits and paint. These processes required their own equipment which made an oil works look like a huge outdoor laboratory with stills, tanks, condensers, aspirators and other apparatus connected by miles of pipes and plumbing. The picture shows a bench of crude oil coking stills which were used to extract the last drop of oil and in the process turn the residue into coke which had to be removed with picks by men wearing wooden clogs to withstand the heat and the corrosive nature of the material.

Paraffin wax, always an important product of the industry, was extracted from crude oil after its second distillation. Having been cooled to atmospheric temperatures the oil was passed through tube-like coolers and then pumped into a filter press, seen in the picture on the left, to form caked paraffin. This still held a lot of oil which was removed by the hydraulic presses in the picture on the right. These were loaded in much the same way as a cider press with trays of solid paraffin interspersed with cloth. After some hours in the press the blocks of paraffin were removed, melted and stored ready for refining. Known as scale, the crude solid paraffin wax was then submitted to a process known as sweating, in oven-like houses which removed residual oil. By carefully adjusting the oil content the colour and melting point of the wax could be controlled and different products created. The colour could also be adjusted by a final filtration process. The principal use of the wax was to make candles.

Throughout its existence the industry had a problem that got bigger by the day – the bings. There was no obvious use for spent shale, although some attempts had been made to mix it with clay to make bricks. These had generally proved unsuccessful, but the idea of making bricks never went away and after some years of experimentation a solution was found in the 1930s. Pulverised waste shale was mixed with hydrated lime and lime slurry and fed into a brick moulding machine. The formed bricks were then, as seen here, loaded onto bogies and wheeled into steam-heated ovens known as autoclaves, where they were hardened. A distinctive pink colour, SOL bricks (the initials of Scottish Oils Limited) were very good and were widely used for buildings throughout the shale industry and at the Grangemouth refinery. They were also used for stoppings, shaft linings and other purposes in the mines, but they made little difference to the size of the bings.

School boards, set up under the provisions of the Education Act of 1872, were required to ensure that all children between the ages of five and thirteen went to school. This tricky task was compounded for boards in sparsely populated rural areas by the sudden arrival of a large industry. The big concerns recognised that they had a responsibility, indeed some company schools had existed before the legislation, and although the Pumpherston company was formed after the act came into force, they erected a school building (opened in September 1886) and leased it to the Mid-Calder School Board. Starting with 125 pupils the school roll rose inexorably over the years, creating the need for extensions to the original building and the occasional use of the neighbouring institute hall which is on the left of this early twentieth century view of the school. The institute was also built by the company and like all such places became a centre for social life in the village and a place of continuing learning because one of its facilities was a library and reading room, the classic poor man's university.

THE CO-OPERATIVE BUILDINGS PUMPHERSTON

Another focus of village life was the co-operative store, better known as the store. Prior to its opening villagers were served by a small shop which, although on company premises, was not a company shop so there was no restriction on co-op vans coming in and doing a roaring trade. Encouraged by this business, and indications that the oil works might be around for a while, the West Calder Co-operative Society opened a branch in the village in 1887. Founded on the principles established by the Rochdale Equitable Pioneers Society, whereby members shared in profits through the distribution of a dividend, the Pumpherston branch grew in size, with most village households signed up as members. As trade boomed the buildings were extended a couple of times and the product range expanded to include groceries, bread, meat, clothes, shoes and explosives. That last item might seem unusual, but miners had to provide their own equipment so gunpowder was a necessity, although it was not sold over the counter with food, but in a hut some distance away from this imposing building erected in 1900.

There must have been something in the air in 1883 with six oil companies being established. One of these, the Bathgate Oil Company, set up its works at Seafield, but was soon in financial difficulties and was taken over in 1891 by another of those 1883 start-ups, the Pumpherston Oil Company. They erected a new bench of retorts in 1895 and later installed three benches of state-of-the-art Bryson, or Pumpherston, retorts. This reconstruction gave Seafield works a new lease of life and it remained operational until 1931. The company also built more houses in the adjacent village. Straddling the Whitburn to Livingstone road, Seafield originally consisted of five rows of 24 houses, with three rows on one side of the road and two on the other. In three of the rows the houses consisted of a room and kitchen with an added scullery and toilet. The houses in another row also had gardens and those in the fifth row an attic room and a garden.

Another 1883 newcomer, the West Lothian Oil Company, was greeted with scepticism by the local newspaper, the West Lothian Courier, which suggested that investors should avoid it and put their money into other ventures. But the company raised its capital and erected an oil works at Deans, just over a couple of miles to the east of Seafield. Perhaps the paper was right because the company struggled, making frequent changes to management and working methods, and eventually gave up in 1891. The works and mines lay abandoned until 1894 when they were taken over by the Pumpherston Oil Company who installed three benches, one of 68 retorts, the others with 52 each. Oil production restarted in 1896. A major upgrade of the works, including the addition of 156 retorts in three benches, was carried out in 1908. Deans was now one of the largest crude oil works in the industry and indeed for a time under Scottish Oils it was the biggest. It closed in 1946.

In taking over the Deans works and mines, the Pumpherston Oil Company inherited some housing, but it was poor quality and insufficient, so they created a new village for their employees at Livingston Station. Built in blocks of six or eight and arranged in rows, like the one shown here, there were initially about 160 dwellings, roughly half of which comprised a room and kitchen while the others also had attic rooms. Sculleries and toilets were added later. With little gardens to the front and larger ones to the rear, these houses compared favourably with others in the industry, but there was nothing else in the village, only houses. This is the way it was for rural communities attached to extractive industries, because public authorities were reluctant to invest in infrastructure and traders preferred to operate from vans until the venture looked as if it was going to be around for a while. The West Calder Co-operative Society took the plunge in late March 1904 when it opened a branch store. A year later it opened a hall and a couple of years after that, a bakery.

The facilities at Livingston Station were expanded in October 1906 when the Pumpherston Oil Company opened a new institute. It had a 250 seat hall, with stage and retiring rooms, and there was also a smaller hall intended as a recreation room, library and anteroom to the large hall. Dances, weddings and social functions of all kinds were expected to take place in the new institute, but in a village with no church, so too were religious services, Sunday School, Band of Hope meetings and Gospel readings. The formation of a literary and debating society was also anticipated in response to the provision of a library. Having built the institute, the company handed it over to a committee of local people to manage. A bowling green was opened alongside in 1908. It must have irked the Co-op to have its hall so quickly trumped by this new rival, but it was able to provide classroom accommodation for village children for whom there was nowhere else to go for lessons until a purpose-built school was opened in March 1909. The institute, seen here in a picture from about the 1940s, was later enlarged to include a billiard room and spray baths (showers).

The company of Meldrum, McLagan & Simpson (Edward Meldrum was one of James Young's original partners at Bathgate), opened an oil works at Uphall in 1866. They set up the Starlaw Oil Works the following year to supply crude oil to the Uphall refinery, but disaster struck at the adjacent Starlaw Pit in 1870 when a ventilation furnace set the wooden shaft lining alight. The winding engineman, at great risk to himself, broke every rule in the book in a heroic attempt to get the 56 men and boys to the surface, but seven didn't make it and one rescued man was so badly injured he also died. It was one of the worst pit disasters in the shale industry. The following year the proprietors formed the Uphall Mineral Oil Company, but struggled to get it onto a sound footing and in 1884 amalgamated with Young's Paraffin Light and Mineral Oil Company. The Starlaw works had already ceased operations, but Young's upgraded crude oil production and refining capacity at Uphall. After 1921 the plant was used by Scottish Oils to refine imported crude oil brought from Grangemouth initially by rail and, from 1924, by a newly installed pipeline. Uphall closed in 1936.

When the Anglo Persian Oil Company's subsidiary, Scottish Oils, took on the overall management of the shale companies they established their headquarters at Middleton Hall, a grand mansion set in private wooded grounds at Uphall. The house was originally built about 1700, but the Earls of Buchan carried out modifications in the later eighteenth century that were so extensive little of the early structure was recognisable when Scottish Oils moved in. They made further changes, tacking on extensions and converting it into offices, laboratories and workshops. Perhaps the biggest change wrought by the company was to the estate, which they transformed about 1924 by building a large number of houses for their employees. Ranging from four in a block flatted dwellings to these large semi-villas in Westhall Gardens, it is hard to believe that such houses were created by the same industry that only a few years earlier had been responsible for some of the old rows.

If James Young has received scant recognition, history has almost wholly overlooked the part played by Robert Bell in developing the oil industry. He had taken a lease on minerals in the Broxburn area, but instead of coal he found lots of shale. The hitherto worthless mineral was beginning to attract interest and Young had started to experiment with it at Bathgate, but when Bell set up a works at Broxburn in 1861 it was the first to produce oil from shale. In order to attend to other interests he leased the works, and supplied shale to a number of small local works that had also started up, but these disparate concerns amounted to little until in 1877 they were all were combined into a single entity, the Broxburn Oil Company. Bell played a big part in the company's formation and was a principal shareholder in what was to become one of the most important shale oil operations. The works is seen here about 1910 looking south to the town. Bell also claimed responsibility for another of the industry's successes. Observing that vegetation flourished where ammonia was discharged as waste into water courses, he concluded that it could be used as a fertiliser, and the highly profitable production of sulphate of ammonia was begun.

As ever the success or failure of a venture depended on people and at Broxburn one of the most influential was works manager Norman Henderson. Recruited from the Oakbank Oil Company, where he had designed a new type of retort, Henderson rebuilt and unified the works. He erected new benches of retorts on the south side of the Union Canal at the Albyn works and linked this by pipeline to the refinery on the north bank of the canal. If by splitting the works the canal compromised their efficiency, the industry's impact on the canal was disappointingly slight. Built between 1818 and 1822 the canal was intended to shake up the corrupt Edinburgh coal trade, which it did, but was then rendered obsolete by railways. A major industry springing up on the banks could therefore have changed its fortunes, but sadly the oil men made little use of the canal and its principal value was as a source of water to put out fires, which occurred quite often at Broxburn. Once the largest works in the industry, the Broxburn refinery and Albyn works closed in 1927. The separate Roman Camp crude oil works, to the south of the town, remained in production until 1956.

Greendykes Rows, the largest group of oil works houses in Broxburn, sat on either side of Greendykes Road which runs almost due north from The Cross. It is seen here with refinery chimneys poking above the roofs on the left and the Albyn works bing on the extreme right. The bulk of the 300 houses were situated to the west, behind those on the left of the picture. Young's Paraffin Light and Mineral Oil Company also owned a few one room houses in Greendykes Road. Just before Christmas in 1920 the southern end of Greendykes Road was the scene of spectacular fire that destroyed the headquarters building of the Broxburn Co-operative Society. At the height of the blaze the stone frontage crashed into the road narrowly missing the watching crowd. The following morning, Christmas Eve, supplies were rushed in from the Scottish Co-operative Wholesale Society at Leith and a temporary store opened in Broxburn Public Hall. The only Co-op building to survive was the bakery, an irony because it had been the only part of the Co-op destroyed in another fire in 1907.

New Holygate, a development of 48 Broxburn Oil Company houses, is seen on the right of this view from the canal bridge. There were another 66 houses at Old Holygate, tucked in behind the buildings on the extreme left, between the Port Buchan canal basin and the Catholic church of St. John Cantius and St. Nicholas, identifiable by its prominent spire. A sanitary inspector's report in 1911 was critical of Old Holygate. The houses failed to meet the standards of the day, there were no wash houses, three ash pits for rubbish and fourteen privvies (one for every five families and no separation for male and female use). There was nowhere for storage of coal; some tenants had made their own bunkers, but others kept coal under the beds. Despite these failings there was always a demand for the houses because of a general shortage. The area was also served for a time by a local co-operative society which was set up about 1888, but amalgamated with the Broxburn Co-operative Society after 1901.

A third group of Broxburn Oil Company houses was situated a few hundred yards to the east of Greendykes Road. Known as Stewartfield Rows they were almost cradled by the Albyn crude oil works bing, a location that even the most inventive estate agent would have had difficulty putting a gloss on. They consisted of 92 houses in eleven blocks. Some of the houses were single apartment and some of these were built back to back; there were also some two apartment room and kitchen houses. The report into the state of shale workers' housing in 1914 was scathing about the company's efforts to raise sanitary standards at these rows and stated bluntly that some newly installed toilets should be condemned. Nine had been put against the gables of two blocks of houses, allowing for one between two families, but because the toilets faced each other there was neither privacy nor decency.

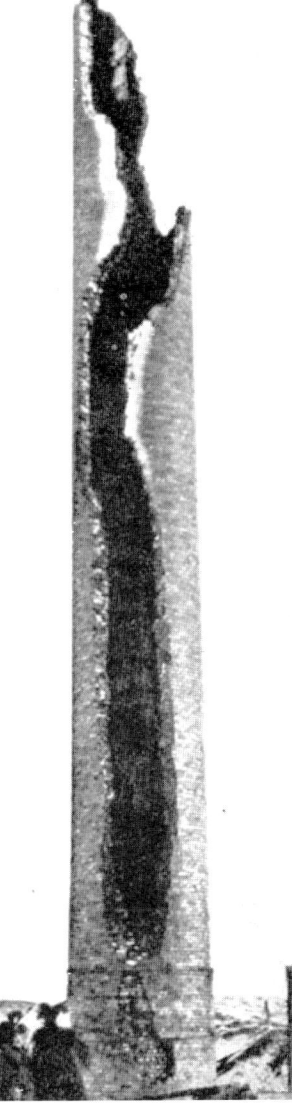

Shale workings were rarely level as this early twentieth century picture of a Broxburn mine shows. In the top left corner a man is boring a shot hole with a rickety, so called because of the noise made by a ratchet that allowed the miner to operate the drill from one side. A large prop is used to give it purchase. The men are using naked flame tallow (or tally) lamps so they would have had to be careful because Broxburn mines were known to be fiery. One such mine was Hayscraigs, also known as Pyothall No. 5, but it wasn't an underground explosion that rocked the mine on 17th January 1910, but a lightning strike. The 130 foot high haulage engine chimney had the side ripped out and about 30 feet knocked off the top. Often the tallest object in the countryside, mine chimneys were prone to this kind of damage, although this one was hit hard. The engineman was knocked off his seat as the lightning travelled from the engine house and into the mine before earthing on a haulage rope guide wheel. Two men working in the mine were knocked off their feet. Within a week two iron tubes had been erected as a temporary chimney, allowing nearly 300 men to return to work. Hayscraigs was one of the largest mines operated by the Broxburn Oil Company, but by June 1919, when its closure was announced, it employed fewer than 100.

41

Shale is a hard rock that cannot be cut with a pick so it had to be broken with explosives to get it out. Shale miners were therefore acutely aware of the dangers associated with blasting and while such a hazardous activity inevitably resulted in accidents these were few compared to the numbers of shots being fired. The workable shale seams tended to be quite thick, so men could stand up rather than having to contend with the cramped conditions of many coal mines. The principal seams were often found close to the surface and were worked from drift mines, like the one in this picture, thought to be Kirkland or Glendevon Mine. Shale mines usually operated on the stoop and room method of working whereby miners took out criss-crossing roadways to the boundary of the area to be worked, leaving large blocks of shale supporting the roof. These were then taken out allowing the roof to collapse behind the working area, creating a void that often caused subsidence on the surface.

The proximity of shale to the surface in many places meant that the practice of extracting it from opencast workings had been fairly widespread in the early years of the industry. Then it was a laborious pick and shovel operation, but at the latter end of the Second World War, with a pressing need to increase the amount of shale being mined, large machines were employed. One of the sites was at Glendevon where this dragline removed the surface deposits to expose the shale which was then taken out using the mechanical shovel. A local reporter who visited the site in March 1945 described the machines as giants . . . tearing and scooping at the earth and transforming the field into a miniature mountain range (with) great heaps of earth . . . intersected with gullies and channels. The extracted shale was taken by lorry to the oil works and the site reinstated by bulldozer.

The Niddry oil works, later renamed Hopetoun oil works, was set up by the Uphall Mineral Oil Company in 1872. It was sited to the south of Winchburgh, to exploit the Camps and Dunnet seams in the Newliston shalefield, and was taken over by Young's Paraffin Light and Mineral Oil Company along with the rest of the Uphall company's assets in 1884. Only ever a crude oil works it was re-equipped with Young and Beilby retorts in the late 1880s. These were superseded at the start of the twentieth century by an improved version developed in collaboration between the company's managing director, William Fyfe, and the original designer, William Young. The construction of more Young and Fyfe retorts, in 150 foot long benches, is seen here in 1906. With the industry struggling in the early 1920s the works' future looked to be in doubt, but it survived for two more decades until closing in 1946.

Oakbank Oil Works   Winchburgh

In 1900 the Oakbank Oil Company took out a 31 year lease on the shale, on land between Winchburgh and the Firth of Forth belonging to Hopetoun Estate. Test bores proved positive and the company opened new mines near Duddingston to work the rich Dunnet seam. At Winchburgh they erected a new oil works and named it Niddry Castle, after the nearby stronghold of the Seaton family where Mary Queen of Scots sheltered in 1568, after her escape from Loch Leven Castle. The new works was equipped with Pumpherston retorts capable of dealing with 500 tons of shale a day. It was started up in 1903, the first completely new development in the industry for over a decade. What marked the whole operation out from its predecessors was the use of electricity, not just at the works, but in the mines and the railway linking the mines to the oil works.

The two foot six inch gauge railway that ran between the Duddingston mines and the Niddry Castle works was the first to be operated by electricity in Scotland. Two American power units were used at first, although later locomotives were British, including one built by Andrew Barclay of Kilmarnock. The line was initially just over two miles long, but was shortened by a few hundred yards after the closure of Duddingston No. 1 Mine in 1941. A two mile long spur was made to the west in the 1920s, to connect the line to Philpstoun Nos. 1 and 6 Mines, and a shorter spur was made to the Totleywells Mine, to the east, in 1938. Cable haulage was used on these spurs. Men travelling to and from the mines also used the trains and although closed wagons were provided for them, most preferred to sit on the shale tubs. This had its dangers as one man discovered in 1920 when he was hit and injured by the trolley pole after it became detached from the overhead wire. The electric line remained in use up to the closure of Niddry Castle works in 1961.

Winchburgh was a village of fewer than 100 dwellings before the Niddry Castle oil works was set up, but it trebled in size when the Oakbank Oil Company erected over 200 houses for their employees. Arguably the best houses built for shale workers before the First World War, most of these had three rooms of dimensions that would not be unusual in modern developments. They had a sink, toilet, coal cellar and a scullery with clothes washing facilities. There were drying greens, but no gardens. Other houses were of two apartments, or room and kitchen, but with the same sanitary facilities as the larger dwellings. There was proper drainage, a good water supply and refuse was put out in bins and collected three times a week, a far cry from the dry privvies or communal toilets and open ash pits of other villages. Electricity from the works power plant was used for street lighting between the rows. This picture, taken from the Hopetoun oil works bing, shows the rows when new with the Niddry Castle oil works on the extreme right. The Union Canal runs across the foreground in a tree-lined cutting.

In February 1903, with Niddry Castle works nearing completion and people moving into the new rows, the Broxburn Co-operative Society opened a branch store in Winchburgh's Main Street. Designed by the architects of the Scottish Co-operative Wholesale Society the new store, on the right of this picture, was the society's first outside their home town. The president of the society, Mr. Chambers, stood on the tray of a lorry (presumably like the one in the picture), to perform the opening ceremony. After the speeches trading began and the official party returned to their Broxburn headquarters for a celebratory tea. The Broxburn Co-operative Society had a few ups and downs and on a couple of occasions explored the possibility of amalgamation with West Calder, the other big co-operative society in the shale working areas. Nothing came of these initiatives, but in November 1968, with the shale industry receding into history, the Broxburn and Bathgate societies merged to form the West Lothian Co-operative Society and this amalgamated with West Calder in 1979.

The picture on the facing page, which dates from no later than 1904, shows Main Street as an unhurried thoroughfare, but out of sight on the ground behind the co-op and adjoining buildings there was, as these two pictures show, a lot of effort being put into providing a range of produce. A variety of installations including a chicken run, vegetable plots and potting sheds have been created to utilise every inch of ground. These plots were perhaps a little more extensive than the allotments that were generally popular in mining and industrial communities. In the background of the vertical picture are the shale workers' rows erected by the Oakbank Oil Company. The space in between has since been filled with council housing.

High on the list of social facilities deemed desirable or even essential to village life was the bowling green, so the formal opening of the Oakbank Workmens' (Winchburgh) Bowling Green, in August 1913, was a moment of some celebration. It helped that the weather was fine. The Marchioness of Linlithgow was unable to attend, so Mrs Thomson, wife of Alexander Cunningham Thomson of the Oakbank Company, threw the first jack and the Marquis of Linlithgow rolled the first bowl to within a foot of it. Giving a speech after this feat of sporting prowess, the Marquis dismissed it as a lucky shot and suggested he would probably miss the entire green if asked to throw another bowl. He ended by formally declaring the green open. A committee of local men had been responsible for the project and through subscriptions, and fund-raising with a bazaar and sale of work, had met most of the cost by the time the green opened. Since then the little pavilion in this picture has been superseded by more modern facilities and the name has changed to Winchburgh Bowling Club.

Fifty years separate the picture on page 47 and this one taken from a similar point in 1954. The rows are still there, but Winchburgh has expanded with the addition of council housing, notably in the left foreground. With the Hopetoun works having closed eight years earlier its bing has stopped growing, but Niddry Castle is still working and the substantial bing it has built up, on the right of the picture, has a few more years worth of spent shale to be added. Throughout its operational life Niddry Castle was regarded as an efficient works. It was extended in 1907 with additional retorts, naphtha plant, boilers and generators. A new mine, Duddingston No. 3, was opened to the south of the existing mines and 200 extra miners were employed to supply the shale needed to keep the new plant working. When times were tough in the inter-war years, the works was retained while others were shut down, but in November 1960 Scottish Oils had to bow to the inevitable and announce the closure of Niddry Castle.

James Ross and Company, a chemical manufacturer based beside the Forth & Clyde Canal at Lime Wharf, Falkirk (where the Falkirk Wheel is now sited) obtained a lease of minerals from the Earl of Hopetoun and in 1883 set up the Philpstoun Oil Works. The site between the Union Canal and the Edinburgh and Glasgow Railway was ideal for transport links, but a bit restricted for the disposal of spent shale. The bottom right corner of this view is filled by the North Bing, behind it are the retorts and leading from them is a hutch road that crosses the canal in the lower left corner to the South Bing from where the picture was taken. The huge bings effectively created a deep canyon with the canal at the bottom, which had its drawbacks as your scribe discovered when, during a boat race in 1979, the outboard engine propeller hit a submerged block of solidified shale from one of the bings and broke the shear pin! Philpstoun works was initially equipped with Henderson retorts, although these were later replaced by a locally modified version of Young and Beilby retorts.

USE ROSS PETROL

!!! This is The Best and Most Economical Motor Spirit in the Market, and it is Home Made.

ROSS PETROL

Manufactured by
JAMES ROSS & Cº., Philpstoun Oil Works, Linlithgow, NB

W & A K Johnston Limited Edinburgh & London.

In 1884, the year after Philpstoun was set up, the newly formed Linlithgow Oil Company, started an oil works at Bridgend to exploit shales from the Champfleurie Estate. Being so close to each other there was great rivalry between the people of Philpstoun and Bridgend, but the latter works was poorly managed and, with the company slow to accept the need to modernise its Henderson retorts, it went out of business in 1902. James Ross and Company moved quickly to acquire the mineral assets, re-employed the miners, and took on others from the Bridgend workforce at Philpstoun. With 352 retorts in six benches retorting 850 tons of shale a day Philpstoun was regarded as a major producer of crude oil, naphtha and sulphate of ammonia. As this advertisement card shows James Ross also made petrol, but ironically, with car ownership growing, the Philpstoun works closed in 1931. Scottish Oils continued to make petrol, branded as Scotch petrol, at Pumpherston.

Presiding over the growing works village was the manager's house, Castlepark, built in 1896 interestingly some time after housing had been provided for the workforce. The first occupant was Archibald Crichton who ruled like a landed laird allocating houses, settling disputes, advising on lifestyle, and also, because he was a skilled mining engineer, running the entire works operation above and below ground. He was succeeded by his son Robert who, like his father, was a mining engineer, steeped in the oil industry. As well as being manager of the Philpstoun works, Bob Crichton was given wider responsibilities with Scottish Oils when it took over the whole industry. He is credited with implementing a pioneering work-share scheme known as spread over which employed men three weeks out of four, thus keeping them in jobs and retaining their skills until the good times returned. An interesting feature of Castlepark is the large thistle set above the windows on the left. Its significance, if any, is not known, but a thistle shape was adopted for the tops of Scotch petrol pumps.

With a pick over his shoulder and a carbide lamp on his cap, a young miner stands proudly on a cart carrying sacks of sulphate of ammonia and a model of James Ross & Co.'s Philpstoun oil works. It is hauled by a beautifully presented Clydesdale horse that has just been awarded a first prize. Where this victory was won is not known, but it could have been at an event like the annual West Lothian Agricultural Show which included a category for horses in harness. There was also a competition for pit ponies that attracted entries from the major oil companies. James Ross & Co., in common with the other big companies, took a paternalistic interest in the social welfare of their employees and provided an institute at Philpstoun, and ensured that people would use it by taking a small levy from every wage packet to pay for it. Dances, concerts and other social functions were held at the institute while villagers also took part in a variety of outdoor social and sporting activities.

DALMENY OIL WORK.

SOUTH QUEENSFERRY.

The shalefield outcropped in Fife where it was worked with moderate success at Binnend near Burntisland between 1878 and 1895. A more significant outlier was Clippens oil works at Straiton, Midlothian, which was an industry leader until a dispute with the Edinburgh and District Water Trustees forced its closure in 1898. The longest lasting works in the north east of the field was therefore the one established by the Dalmeny Oil Company in 1871. It only ever operated as a crude works, sending oil to Oakbank to be refined, and having re-equipped with Pumpherston retorts in 1899 was ticking along nicely when serious geological problems brought its mines to a halt. New mines were opened, but the shale was inferior and although supplies from elsewhere kept the works going for a while, closure was announced in July 1926. The works was dismantled, but after the discovery of North Sea oil in the 1970s, a tank farm, screened by a bund of spent shale from the old bing, was built on the site. The oil was brought ashore and treated at the Kinneil gas separation plant at the Grangemouth refinery, before being piped to the Dalmeny storage tanks and on to a tanker loading jetty in the Forth.